Zen and Western Philosophy

Philosophers' Ideas in Haiku

Stan Baronett

ALINEA

Alinea Learning

ALINEA

Alinea Learning

Boston, Massachusetts

Published in the United States by Alinea Learning, an imprint and division of Alinea Knowledge, LLC, Boston.

Visit our website at www.alinealearning.com.

Library of Congress Cataloging-in-Publication Data is available on file.

Print book ISBN: 979-8-9878531-3-9

eBook ISBN: 979-8-9878531-4-6

Preface

This is an attempt to capture the body of thought called "Western philosophy" with an Eastern net—Zen as embodied in haiku. It offers profiles of Western philosophers by using a three-line format of 5-7-5 syllables to capture each philosopher's ideas in a manner that is concise and playful. It is an exercise by someone schooled in Western philosophy to see things from a different perspective. The book's purpose, design, and structure is

A parallax view

of Western philosophy

through an Eastern lens.

Contents

Thales

All things are water.
Natural explanation;
no need for old gods.

Pythagoras

Stardust, sea urchins,

every cell inside your brain;

their base is number.

Heraclitus

A hungry fish jumps.
It splashes back into a
different river.

Zeno of Elea

Achilles gets near
but cannot pass the tortoise.
Motion illusion.

Socrates

**The reflecting pond
waits silently while the man
examines his life.**

Democritus

Mount Athos, full of
indivisible atoms,
and yet change happens.

Plato

Shadows are all things
to those chained in the dark cave.
Sunlight waits outside.

Aristotle

Flowers eat the sun,
always in moderation,
enough to live right.

Epicurus

**When we exist, death
is not here. When it comes,
we no longer exist.**

Euclid

Silky spider-webs:
Geometry's axioms
in three dimensions.

Archimedes

I slip into a

soothing warm bath. The liquid

displaced. Eureka!

Chrysippus of Soli

If this is my child,

then I have found my way home.

Yes, this is my child.

Epictetus

Wealth consists not in having great possessions, but in having few wants.

Marcus Aurelius

The goal of seeking rational understanding is to change our lives.

Augustine of Hippo

**The holy person
rejects earthly pleasures in
the City of God.**

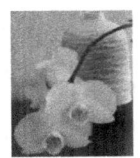

Anselm of Canterbury

Consider God as
that which nothing greater can
ever be conceived.

Thomas Aquinas

Rain wets the young rose.
The universe being pushed
by the prime mover.

William of Ockham

Too much confusion
strangles my new ideas.
Get a sharp razor.

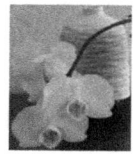

Jean Buridan

The ass stands between
two tempting bales of fresh hay.
The ass cannot choose.

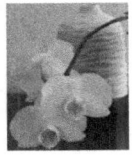

Niccolò Machiavelli

**Kings of the jungle
rule by guile and fear; the ends
justify the means.**

Copernicus

Spiders spin on a
spinning globe that clings to the
Sun at the center.

Michel de Montaigne

Do not tie yourself

to simply one principle.

Free your thoughts and soar.

Giordano Bruno

You who pronounce my
death sentence fear it more than
I who receive it.

Francis Bacon

Twelve dogs sniff around,
while scientists parse data
and generalize.

Galileo Galilei

"Earth is the center!"
shouts the Church. *(Nevertheless,*
I know the Earth moves.)

Thomas Hobbes

Venus flytraps, men,

and dogs live in a brave world—

nasty, brutish, short.

René Descartes

The cold lake at night
slaps my face and wakens me.
I think, thus I am.

Pierre de Fermat

A clever theorem.
I have a proof, but not the
time or space. Later.

Blaise Pascal

A fading cleric,

a dying clerk, make final

wagers. God's gamblers.

Margaret Cavendish

A double knowledge,
rational and sensitive;
thus mind and body.

Anne Conway

**Spirit and body
differ not essentially;
they are the same thing.**

John Locke

Pristine snow. New-born
baby. Pure blank slates upon
which all is written.

Baruch Spinoza

Gaze at a snowflake.
Nature or God? It depends
on your perspective.

Nicolas Malebranche

**The wind blows, the leaf
falls, on the occasion of
God's activity.**

Isaac Newton

Gravity charming
an apple, an orchard, and
a grizzled farmer.

Gottfried Leibniz

A water lily,

a fat green frog. The best of

all possible worlds.

Damaris Masham

The only grounds of
virtue are religion and
a deep fear of God.

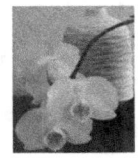

Mary Astell

Opinion: Myself.

Science: Distinct ideas.

Authority: Faith

George Berkeley

An idea of
a slate grey stone, inside my
mind, inside God's mind.

Voltaire

No authority

can be immune from reason.

Apply it always.

Thomas Bayes

A way to test your
epistemic confidence:
My complex theorem.

Leonhard Euler

**Interlocked circles
can reveal the logic of
class relationship.**

David Hume

Two kinds of knowledge: Relations of Ideas and Matters of Fact.

Jean-Jacques Rousseau

The state of nature,
to what end? Man, born free, but
everywhere in chains.

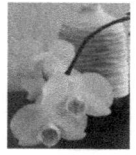

Adam Smith

**Self-preservation
and competition creates
the wealth of nations.**

Paul-Henri d'Holbach

We are physical.

Free will is an illusion.

Choice? Causal forces.

Immanuel Kant

Discarded snake skin.

A lover's eyes peering deep.

The thing-in-itself.

Catharine Macaulay

Abuse of power?

Social contract corrupted?

Form new government.

Cesare Beccaria

Punishment should be swift and consistent, only to deter others.

William Paley

Consider a watch.

Design needs a designer.

God designs all things.

Jeremy Bentham

**Pollen-laden bees
darting home; sweet honey for
the greatest number.**

Pierre-Simon Laplace

**What we know is not
much. What we do not know is
immense. Get to work.**

Johann Goethe

The world is empty

if you know only rivers.

Strive to know someone.

Mary Wollstonecraft

**Women should have rights
in common with men, equal
in every sense.**

Thomas Malthus

Population growth—
geometric; but food growth—
arithmetic. Death.

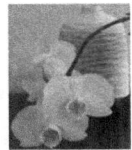

Georg Hegel

Thesis: A subject.

Antithesis: An object.

Synthesis: Spirit.

Mary Shepherd

Sensations of a
continuous existence:
It's the unperceived.

Bernard Bolzano

Object 1: A dog.

Object 2: Numbers and sets.

Both of these exist.

Arthur Schopenhauer

An owl and a child—
actors in a world—*will* and
representation.

William Whewell

I propose to call
natural philosophers
"scientists" instead.

John Stuart Mill

Ants serve wordlessly.
Yet humans need free speech and
social liberty.

Augustus De Morgan

Develop logic.

Transform thoughts into symbols,

then you can advance.

Charles Darwin

Parasitic wasps

devour caterpillars from

within—God's design?

Søren Kierkegaard

A sudden shake, fear
and trembling arising with
every choice I make.

George Boole

Rules of logic and
symbol manipulation:
That's formalism.

Augusta Ada Byron

**The power of an
analytical engine:
An algorithm.**

Henry David Thoreau

Deep in woods, I seek
not love, not money, not fame;
I seek only truth.

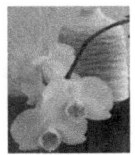

Karl Marx

Tired huddled masses.

Religion, the opium

of the scared masses.

Thomas H. Huxley

Ethical process:

Not the strongest, but the ones

ethically the best.

Lewis Carroll

Curious. You used

to be much more muchier.

You lost your muchness.

John Venn

A syllogism.
Use interlocking circles—
Valid, Invalid?

Ernst Mach

**Metaphysical
elements destroy science.
Eliminate them.**

Charles Sanders Peirce

Apply abduction.
Seek a hypothesis that
accounts for the facts.

William James

**A river's blooming
buzzing confusion flows to
a calm pool of thought.**

Friedrich Nietzsche

An old fly lands on
a poised thief, freely choosing—
yes, all gods are dead.

Christine Ladd-Franklin

Negate conclusion.

Now, if inconsistent with

premises: Valid.

Gottlob Frege

"Mount Fuji, tallest
in Japan." See the mountain,
understand the sense.

Hans Vaihinger

Theories are useful,
but false. The philosophy
of "As If" writ large.

Sigmund Freud

Black falcon—the stuff
of dreams—and a treasure chest
of wish-fulfillment.

Thorstein Veblen

Cheap labor and goods.

Conspicuous consumption.

Thus, the leisure class.

Edmund Husserl

**Build the science of
Intentionality—the
seat of consciousness.**

Henri Bergson

Comedy's function?
Laughter. A social gesture
that's strictly human.

John Dewey

**Democracy is
a way of life—social and
individual.**

Alfred N. Whitehead

**The aim of science
is to seek simplicity,
but then distrust it.**

Pierre Duhem

**Background assumptions
hide in an isolated
hypothesis test.**

George Santayana

Primates in long johns,
forgetting the past, doomed to
repeating mistakes.

J. M. E. McTaggart

The past, present, and future lives of a squirrel jointly contradict.

Bertrand Russell

Think of the set of
all sets that are not members
of themselves. What then?

G. E. Moore

The ripe red apple
in my right hand—and look, here
 is another one.

Albert Einstein

The reason for time?
So that everything does not
happen all at once.

Moritz Schlick

Philosophy's task:

The meaning of a statement.

Science's task: Truth.

Otto Neurath

**Like sailors on the
open sea, we reconstruct
our ship from its parts.**

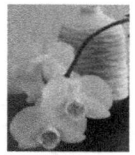

Ludwig Wittgenstein

The thrush sings at dawn.

I cannot say what it means.

Remain silent then.

Martin Heidegger

**Why are there beings
at all instead of nothing?
That is the question.**

Rudolf Carnap

**Pseudo-sentence: An
empty phrase; must verify
all propositions.**

Hans Reichenbach

Mathematical

axioms: Definitions—

neither true nor false.

Susanne Langer

A nightingale's song
and human symbols exist
in separate worlds.

Herbert Marcuse

**When engaged in Art
and Philosophy, Mind is
fully realized.**

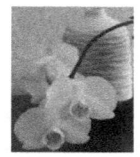

Gilbert Ryle

"A mind must exist!"
No, it's just a fictional
ghost in a machine.

Alfred Tarski

"Snow is white," is true,
if and only if, snow is
white. Nature's wisdom.

Karl Popper

A tangerine seed,
a bold theory, fruitful and
falsifiable.

Frank Ramsey

What we cannot say
we cannot say—and we can't
whistle it either.

Alonzo Church

"Two and two are four"
would be true even if there
were no minds at all.

Carl Hempel

Propositions of mathematics—devoid of factual content.

Jean-Paul Sartre

Science defines rocks.
Humans are self-defined, and
condemned to freedom.

Kurt Gödel

**The best laid formal
systems of mice and men are
ever incomplete.**

Nelson Goodman

**Rules, Intuition,
need to work in reflective
equilibrium.**

Hannah Arendt

**Silent citizens
of corrupt leaders allow
evil to advance.**

Simone de Beauvoir

Not born a woman,

but becomes one outside the

womb—the second sex.

Willard van Orman Quine

A bonsai—to be—
must be the value of a
bound variable.

Gerhard Gentzen

To prove new theorems
use natural deduction:
Forms of argument.

A. J. Ayer

I spent time trying
to make life more rational.
I wasted my time.

J. L. Austin

The more precise you are, the more likely it is that you will be wrong.

Wilfrid Sellars

The two images:

Manifest—Scientific.

Artichokes—Atoms.

Alan Turing

Can a machine think?
Pass the imitation game,
then you can decide.

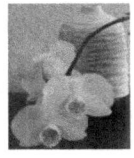

Albert Camus

**I think both that my
life is important and that
life is meaningless.**

Kurt Baier

**Morality gives
reasons that can overrule
our own self-interest.**

Donald Davidson

**Nothing in the world
would be true or false if not
for thinking creatures.**

Raymond Smullyan

Jokes reveal logic:

I would give my right arm to

be ambidextrous.

P. F. Strawson

What is common-sense?
Persons, space, time, causation,
meaning, and truth, too.

Philippa Foot

**Our idea of
human nature is open
to a revision.**

John Rawls

To compete—jungle.

To cooperate—cities.

Justice as fairness.

Thomas Kuhn

Caterpillar, moth;
epicycles or bent space;
paradigm shifting.

Paul Feyerabend

In olden days, truth
and method were quite stable.
Now anything goes.

Hilary Putnam

Thoughts of red roses
need physical red roses,
not brains in a vat.

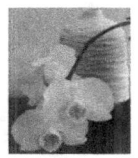

Michel Foucault

Eternal limit:

Power controls and defines

our social knowledge.

Edmund Gettier

Knowledge: *Justified
true belief.* Reasonable?
Sorry, not enough.

Noam Chomsky

**A universal
grammar. Humans do it, and
bees do it. Language.**

Judith Jarvis Thomson

**The right to life is
simply this: The right not to
be killed unjustly.**

Jacques Derrida

**A tension between
a memory and something
absolutely new.**

Richard Rorty

When in harmony,
the given and the mind; a
mirror of nature.

John Searle

Chinese characters
typed on command—syntactics
without semantics.

Ian Hacking

**The best reaction
to a paradox? Invent
a new idea.**

Thomas Nagel

Our lives—serious

or inescapable doubt?

I choose irony.

Robert Nozick

What else matters to us other than how our lives feel from the inside?

Saul Kripke

My dog named "Fido."
Rigid designator in
all possible worlds.

Daniel Dennett

Hunter chases prey.
Belief, intent, and thinking:
Intentional stance.

Patricia Churchland

When *functions* explained,
then *experience* is, too.
Nothing left over.

Peter Singer

Consider the fact:

In suffering, animals

Are equal to us.